THE HIGH PROTEIN COOK
LOUISE KANG
HIGH PROTEIN
SWEET TREATS

Make Your Own Protein Bars, Balls, Pancakes and More

CONTENTS

5.	Introduction
7.	Protein Baking Myths
8.	Protein Rocky Road Brownies
10.	Protein Bounty Bar
12.	Protein Blueberry Cheesecake
14.	Chocolate Protein Truffles
16.	Protein Rocher
18.	Peanut Chocolate Swirl Protein Flapjacks
20.	No Bake Protein Granola Cookies
22.	Protein Birthday Cake
24.	Protein Snickers
26.	Chocolate Protein Lava Cake
28.	Protein Scones
30.	Sweet Potato Protein Brownies
32.	Wongka's Apple, Raisin & Cinnamon Egg Rolls
36.	Salted Caramel Protein Balls
36.	Chocolate Chip Cookie Dough Protein Balls
37.	Chocolate Goji Protein Balls
37.	Superfood Protein Balls
38.	Chocolate Chip Protein Cookies
40.	Protein Mince Pies
42.	Protein Eggnog
44.	Christmas Protein Pancakes
46.	Protein Biscuits
48.	Protein Banana Bread
50.	Protein S'mores in a Mug
52.	Wongka's Salted Chilli-Chocoanana Bites
54.	Protein Ice Cream
56.	Chocolate Protein Crispies
58.	Acknowledgements
59.	Product Recommendations

HIGH PROTEIN SWEET TREATS

Hi and thanks so much for buying my second book.

This book contains 27 delicious recipes made with protein powder.

Baking with protein powder is a trend that has exploded in the past few years. Because so many of us have protein powder in our kitchen cupboards, we are naturally curious to know what else we can do with it.

I used to think that I could simply swap the flour with protein powder in any recipe and it would magically transform into a delicious high protein creation.

Boy was I wrong....

The result was a bland, sponge-like disaster that even my dog wouldn't eat.

Cont:

There are loads of recipes online that include protein powder. But one thing that has always put me off is the need for weird and wonderful types that I'd never heard of. I hate having to fill up my cupboards with bulk packs of ingredients that I'll only ever use once.

For this reason, you will only need **three** kinds of protein powder to make the recipes in this book: **unflavoured whey, vanilla whey and pea protein powder.** (In fact, you don't really need vanilla whey as it's easy to make from unflavoured whey - you just add a little vanilla extract and sweetener.)

You might be wondering why I didn't choose chocolate whey, as most people will have this in their cupboards. The reason is simple: I am yet to find a chocolate-flavoured whey that is good enough. A poor chocolate flavour can ruin your baking, so it's much better to use unflavoured whey with a little good quality cocoa powder and sweetener added.

I hope you enjoy making and eating the treats in this book as much as I did.

Let me know how you get on.

Louise

Louise

www.highproteincook.com
www.facebook.com/highproteincook
www.instagram.com/highproteincook

PROTEIN BAKING MYTHS

You can swap flour for protein powder

No!

Think about it - flour is a grain, while whey (the most common type of protein powder) is a dairy product.

For this reason, whey is going to behave very differently when it reacts with other ingredients in the oven.

Whey goes rubbery and dry when baked

This can be true, especially if you replace flour with whey in any recipe.

BUT it doesn't have to be this way. If you add in some extra 'moist' ingredients, like coconut oil or sweet potato, they will balance out this dryness.

Plant-based protein powders are easier to bake with

This is true – most of the baked recipes in this book include pea protein rather than whey. It's just less likely to result in a dry, rubbery disaster when baked.

Protein treats will never taste as good as the real thing

I disagree – try the Cheesecake on p12 or the Bounty Bars on p10 and hopefully you will feel the same.

RECIPE NOTES

all eggs are medium

any kind of milk can be used (macros are based on semi-skimmed cows milk)

any kind of sugar or sweetener can be used (macros are based on using a low-calorie sweetener rather than sugar)

all chocolate is dark minimum 70% cocoa solids

all US imperial measurements are approximate – use the metric measurements for best results

all macros are approximate and are intended as a guideline only

PROTEIN
ROCKY ROAD BROWNIES

MAKES 12 BROWNIES

20 MINS PREP

2-3 HOURS CHILLING TIME

INGREDIENTS

125g/1¼ cup/5 scoops unflavoured whey protein

2 tbsp cocoa powder

50g/½ cup fine oats

50g/½ cup goji berries

35g/¼ cup chopped nuts

1 tbsp sugar/sweetener

3 tbsp coconut oil

50g/1¾oz dark chocolate

100ml/7 tbsp boiling water

15g/½oz mini marshmallows (optional)

METHOD

1. Add the goji berries and sugar/sweetener into a heatproof bowl together with the hot water. Stir and leave to soak while you prepare the rest of the ingredients.

2. Melt the coconut oil and dark chocolate together in a small saucepan on a very low heat. Leave to cool.

3. Prepare the dry ingredients: add the whey protein, cocoa powder, fine oats and chopped nuts into a large bowl and mix well.

4. Once the goji berries/hot water and chocolate/coconut oil mixtures have cooled, add them both into the large bowl with the dry ingredients. Mix well.

5. Pour the mixture into a brownie tray lined with greaseproof paper.

6. Push the mini marshmallows into the top of the mixture and chill in the fridge for 2 – 3 hours.

7. Remove from the fridge and cut into 12 pieces.

Recipe notes:

- You can add whatever fillings you want to this recipe – whey protein crispies, shortbread pieces and dried fruit all work well.
- Be sure to include some pistachios as they look great when the brownies are sliced.

 153 CALORIES **11g** PROTEIN **11g** FAT **10g** CARBS

MACROS (PER BROWNIE)

PROTEIN
BOUNTY BAR

MAKES 4 BARS

20 MINS PREP
45 MINS CHILLING TIME

INGREDIENTS

50g/½ cup/2 scoops vanilla whey protein

4 tbsp milk

20g/¾oz dessicated coconut, plus a little extra for dusting

2 tbsp coconut oil

40g/1½oz dark chocolate

METHOD

1. Melt the coconut oil and keep aside a teaspoonful for later in the recipe. Mix the rest with the vanilla whey and dessicated coconut.

2. Slowly add the milk. Once the consistency of the mixture is sticky but not too wet, shape into 4 bars on a sheet of greaseproof paper with a little extra desiccated coconut sprinkled over it to make the mixture easier to handle.

3. Put the bars in the fridge for around 30 minutes to set.

4. Meanwhile, melt the chocolate with the remaining coconut oil (add the coconut oil to the pan first so the chocolate doesn't burn).

5. Take the bars out of the fridge and dip in the melted chocolate.

6. Return them to the fridge until the chocolate sets (this should take around 15 minutes).

Recipe notes:

- You can leave out the coconut oil from this recipe and save 60 calories and 7g of fat per bar. However, the texture won't be quite as Bounty-like.

- If you are short of time or very hungry, you can also put the bars in the freezer to set. Just keep an eye on them so they don't freeze completely.

200 CALORIES **11g** PROTEIN **15g** FAT **5g** CARBS

MACROS (PER BAR)

PROTEIN
BLUEBERRY CHEESECAKE

SERVES 8

20 MINS PREP

30 – 40 MINS BAKING

INGREDIENTS

100g/3½oz fruit & nut mix

500g/17½oz 0% fat Greek yoghurt

250g/8¾oz vanilla quark

25g/¼ cup/1 scoop vanilla whey protein

2 eggs

100g/3½oz blueberries

1 tbsp sugar/sweetener

METHOD

1. Preheat the oven to 160°C/320°F.

2. Place the fruit & nut mix in a food processor and blend. Once the mix has become a fine but slightly sticky powder, press it down into the bottom of a 20cm/8" loose base non stick cake tin.

3. Meanwhile, mix together the Greek yoghurt, vanilla quark, vanilla whey and eggs. Spread this mixture over the base.

4. Bake in the oven until the top of the cheesecake is just cooked. This should take 30 – 40 minutes.

5. Meanwhile, place the blueberries in a saucepan together with the sugar/sweetener and heat gently until the berries become soft. Using a spoon or fork, burst the berries and stir until the mixture thickens a little. Remove from the pan and let the mixture cool.

6. Once the cheesecake is done, remove from the oven and let it cool.

7. Once both have cooled down, pour the blueberry topping over the base.

8. Slice into 8 pieces and serve.

Recipe notes:
• If you can't find vanilla quark, you can use unflavoured quark with a teaspoon of vanilla extract and a teaspoon of sugar/sweetener.

• Take care not to overcook the cheesecake.

• Remove it from the oven as soon as the top stops wobbling. It will taste better if slightly undercooked than if overcooked.

158 CALORIES 15g PROTEIN 5g FAT 13g CARBS

MACROS (PER SLICE)

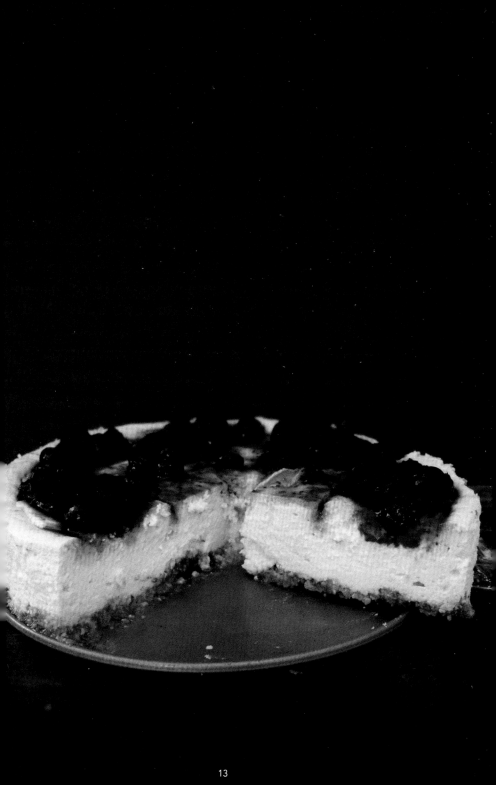

CHOCOLATE PROTEIN TRUFFLES

MAKES 10 TRUFFLES

20 MINS PREP

1 HOUR + CHILLING TIME

INGREDIENTS

25g/1oz dark chocolate

2 tbsp coconut oil

50g/½ cup/2 scoops unflavoured whey protein

1 tsp cocoa powder (+ extra for rolling)

1 tsp sugar/sweetener

3 tbsp milk

METHOD

1. Melt the coconut oil and dark chocolate together carefully in a saucepan on a very low heat. Once melted, let the mixture cool completely.

2. Once cooled, combine with all of the other ingredients. Mix well and leave in the fridge for at least an hour.

3. Now for the messy bit – spoon out a teaspoonful of the mixture and roll into a ball, using a little cocoa powder to cover.

4. Repeat for all 10 truffles.

Recipe notes:
- *For extra creaminess and vitamins, try adding a ripe avocado into the mixture at step 2.*
- *You can flavour the truffles with orange or peppermint oil.....or even some rum.*

60 CALORIES   5g PROTEIN   4g FAT   1g CARBS

MACROS (PER TRUFFLE)

PROTEIN ROCHER

MAKES 14

20 MINS PREP

30 MINS CHILLING TIME

INGREDIENTS

50g/½ cup fine oats

100g/3½oz whey protein crispies

75g/¾ cup/3 scoops vanilla whey protein

100g/½ cup coconut oil

200g/7oz peanut butter

8 crushed malted milk biscuits

100g/3½oz dark chocolate

METHOD

1. Melt the coconut oil in the microwave or on the hob. Keep aside a tablespoonful for step 6.

2. Once melted and cooled, pour the coconut oil into a large bowl along with the other dry ingredients: the oats, whey protein crispies, vanilla whey and crushed biscuits.

3. Add in the peanut butter and stir until everything is combined.

4. Place the bowl in the fridge for 15 minutes to set.

5. Once chilled, remove from the fridge and roll into 14 balls.

6. Carefully melt the chocolate and remaining coconut oil.

7. Coat the balls in the chocolate/oil mixture and place them back in the fridge for another 15 minutes, until the chocolate has set.

Recipe notes:

• This recipe was inspired by a GoNutrition recipe of which I made a video....it was simply too good not to include in the book. It could be easily adapted to lower the fat and calorie content by using less coconut oil and by leaving out the biscuits. The result would be less crunchy but still a yummy treat.

 248 CALORIES
 14g PROTEIN
 19g FAT
 12g CARBS

MACROS (PER BALL)

PEANUT CHOCOLATE SWIRL
PROTEIN FLAPJACKS by Gymster

MAKES 8

30 MINS PREP
15 MINS BAKING
1.5 HOURS CHILLING TIME

INGREDIENTS

200g/7oz peanut butter

100g/3½oz honey

250g/9oz oats

100g/1 cup/4 scoops vanilla whey protein

1 tbsp coconut oil

150ml/²/₃ cup milk

150g/5¹/₃oz dark chocolate

METHOD

1. Preheat the oven to 200°C/390°F.

2. Melt the coconut oil. Mix together with the honey and half of the peanut butter. Make sure everything is melted properly and in liquid form.

3. In a separate bowl, combine the vanilla whey and the milk. Once mixed, add in the coconut oil/honey/peanut butter mixture together with the oats.

4. Flatten the mixture into a baking tray and bake in the oven for 15 minutes. Once done, remove from the oven and leave to cool slightly.

5. Meanwhile, melt the dark chocolate and remaining peanut butter separately (this can be done in the hot oven in two separate dishes).

6. Firstly, pour the melted chocolate over the flapjack base and spread until covered.

7. Secondly, pour the melted peanut butter over the melted chocolate and, using the back of a spoon, mix it around a little to create swirls.

8. Let the flapjacks cool for 30 minutes and place in the fridge for a further hour.

9. Once cooled, cut into 8 slices.

Recipe notes:
* This recipe belongs to my friend Mark Runza. Mark's app, Gymster, has over 170 great recipes like this one. You can download it from the App store and it's available for Android too.

 236 CALORIES
 12g PROTEIN
 12g FAT
21g CARBS

MACROS (PER SLICE)

NO BAKE PROTEIN
GRANOLA COOKIES

MAKES 5

5 MINS PREP
30 MINS CHILLING TIME

INGREDIENTS

50g/1¾oz granola

25g/¼ cup/1 scoop unflavoured whey protein

2 tbsp peanut butter

2 tbsp milk

1 tablespoon coconut flour

METHOD

1. Add the granola, whey protein, coconut flour and peanut butter into a mixing bowl and gradually add in the milk until you get the right texture (i.e. wet enough so that everything sticks together but not too wet).

2. Mix everything together and, using your hands, separate into 5 balls.

3. Flatten each ball into a round cookie shape and put in the fridge to chill for 30 minutes.

Recipe notes:

• *This recipe is so simple and quick.....because the granola is already baked, the finished cookies are crunchy without the need for baking.*

108 CALORIES 7g PROTEIN 6g FAT 7g CARBS

MACROS (PER COOKIE)

PROTEIN BIRTHDAY CAKE

MAKES 12 SLICES

20 MINS PREP
20 MINS BAKING

INGREDIENTS

50g/½ cup/2 scoops unflavoured whey protein powder

2 tsp vanilla extract

3 eggs

150ml/½ cup melted coconut oil

100g/3½oz ground almonds

5 tbsp sugar/sweetener

6 tbsp cocoa powder

100ml/7 tbsp water

1 tsp baking powder

for the icing:

100g/3½oz vanilla quark

25g/¼ cup/1 scoop vanilla whey protein

1 tbsp cocoa powder

METHOD

1. Preheat the oven to 170°C/340°F. Line the base of a 20cm/8" loose base non stick cake tin with greaseproof paper and use a tablespoon or so of the melted coconut oil to grease both the paper and the sides of the tin.

2. Using an electric whisk, beat together the eggs and sugar/sweetener in a large mixing bowl. Once frothy, slowly beat in the remaining coconut oil (make sure it has cooled completely beforehand).

3. Using a wooden spoon, carefully fold in the remaining cake ingredients.

4. Pour the mixture into the cake tin and bake for 20 minutes, or until a cocktail stick comes up clean except for a few chocolate crumbs.

5. Remove from the oven and leave the cake to cool in its tin.

6. Meanwhile, make the icing: using an electric whisk, combine the vanilla quark with the vanilla whey and cocoa powder.

7. Once the cake has cooled, cover in icing and serve.

Recipe notes:

- *This recipe was inspired by Nigella's chocolate olive oil cake. As with Nigella's version, you can swap the almond flour for regular plain flour (use 75g) which will result in it being lighter and more 'cake'-like.*

- *The cake would also be perfect with some icing sugar sprinkled over the top in place of the quark-based icing.*

200 CALORIES | **10g** PROTEIN | **18g** FAT | **6g** CARBS

MACROS
(PER SLICE)

PROTEIN SNICKERS

MAKES 6

20 MINS PREP
40 MINS CHILLING TIME

INGREDIENTS

100g/1 cup/4 scoops vanilla whey
protein

4 tbsp coconut flour (plus a little
extra for dusting)

100ml/7 tbsp milk

6 medjool dates

20g/¾oz chopped mixed nuts

1 tsp salted caramel flavouring

60g/2oz dark chocolate

1 tbsp coconut oil

METHOD

1. Add the vanilla whey and coconut flour into a large mixing bowl and gradually add the milk until you get the right texture of dough (i.e. wet enough so that it sticks together but not too sticky to handle).

2. Separate into 6 equally sized balls and then flatten into bar shapes using your hands. Leave the bars in the fridge to chill a little.

3. To make the topping: remove the stones from the medjool dates and blend together with the salted caramel flavouring in a food processor to make a paste.

4. Spoon the paste over the top of each bar and press some chopped mixed nuts into the top.

5. Using a small saucepan, carefully melt the chocolate and coconut oil together.

6. Remove the bars from the fridge and cover in chocolate. Return them into the fridge to set, which should take a further 30 minutes.

Recipe notes:
- The salted caramel flavouring is optional, but highly recommended. You can also use it to make the salted caramel protein balls on page 36.

 218 CALORIES
 17g PROTEIN
 10g FAT
 16g CARBS

MACROS (PER BAR)

CHOCOLATE PROTEIN
LAVA CAKE

SERVES 2

5 MINS PREP
3 - 5 MINS BAKING

INGREDIENTS

25g/¼ cup/1 scoop unflavoured whey protein

1 tbsp cocoa powder

1 egg

1 tbsp sugar/sweetener

1 tbsp ground almonds

2 tbsp coconut oil

2 tbsp milk

METHOD

1. Preheat the oven to 180°C/350°F. Line the bottom of a ramekin (or two, if you can find very small ones) with greaseproof paper – trace around the outside of the base and cut with scissors to make it fit.

2. Melt the coconut oil and use a teaspoonful to grease the sides of the ramekin(s).

3. Mix the remaining coconut oil with all of the other ingredients in a mixing bowl. Once blended, pour into the ramekin and bake in the hot oven.

4. After 3 minutes, check to see if the top and sides of the cake are fully cooked. If so, it's ready.

5. Using a knife, separate the sides of the cake away from the ramekin. Place an upside-down plate over the ramekin and then flip both. The cake should hopefully fall down onto the plate intact.

6. Peel off the greaseproof paper and serve.

Recipe notes:
- Don't be tempted to leave out the greaseproof paper – the bottom of the cake will stick and it will be impossible to get out.
- This recipe would also make a fantastic mug cake – microwave it for around 30 seconds – 1 minute.

230 CALORIES   14g PROTEIN   19g FAT   3g CARBS

MACROS (PER SERVING)

PROTEIN SCONES

MAKES 5

10 MINS PREP
15 MINS BAKING

INGREDIENTS

125g/4½oz wholemeal self-raising flour
(plus extra for dusting)

50g/1¾oz salted butter

25g/¼ cup/1 scoop vanilla or
unflavoured whey protein (see notes)

70ml/⅓ cup milk

1 egg (optional, for brushing over
the top)

METHOD

1. Preheat the oven to 180°C/350°F. Line a baking tray with some greaseproof paper.

2. Mix together the flour, butter, whey protein and milk to get a soft dough.

3. Turn on to a floured work surface and knead very lightly. Pat down flat until around 2cm thick. Use a 5cm/2in cutter to stamp out rounds and place on the baking tray. Lightly knead together the rest of the dough and stamp out more scones to use it all up.

4. Brush the tops of the scones with the beaten egg. Bake for around 15 minutes until well risen and golden.

Recipe notes:

• For sweet scones, use vanilla whey protein or unflavoured whey plus a little vanilla essence and sugar/sweetener.

• For savoury scones, use unflavoured whey (a pinch of sugar or sweetener will take away the bitterness of the flour). You could even top with some grated cheese.

 180 CALORIES **7g** PROTEIN **9g** FAT **16g** CARBS

MACROS (PER SCONE)

SWEET POTATO
PROTEIN BROWNIES

MAKES 8 BROWNIES

5 MINS PREP

30 MINS BAKING

INGREDIENTS

1 medium sized sweet potato (around 300g/10oz in weight)

100g/3½oz peanut butter

25g/¼ cup/1 scoop unflavoured whey protein

2 tsp cocoa powder

1 tsp sugar/sweetener

25g/1oz chocolate, melted

METHOD

1. Prick the sweet potato all over with a fork and microwave on high for 8 to 10 minutes, turning once. Remove, check that the inside is tender and let it cool.

2. Preheat the oven to 180°C/350°F and grease or line a brownie tin with greaseproof paper.

3. Once cooled, scoop out the inside of the potato and mash until smooth. Add in the peanut butter, whey protein, cocoa powder, sugar/sweetener and melted chocolate. Mix everything together until smooth.

4. Pour the mixture into the brownie tin. Using a fork or spoon, spread the mixture along the whole of the tin, making it level.

5. Bake for around 20 minutes, until the top is well cooked.

6. Remove the brownie tin from the oven, let it cool for a few minutes and then carefully slice into 8 pieces.

Recipe notes:

• Be sure to mash the sweet potato well, breaking it up completely. The last thing you want to find in your brownie is a piece of sweet potato

• You can also peel and cube the sweet potato and cook it in the microwave or in boiling water.

140 CALORIES 7g PROTEIN 8g FAT 12g CARBS

MACROS (PER BROWNIE)

WONGKA'S APPLE, RAISIN & CINNAMON EGG ROLLS

MAKES 4 ROLLS

15 MINS PREP
45 MINS COOKING TIME

INGREDIENTS

2 apples, core removed and chopped

2 tsp coconut oil

1 square lavash bread

4 tbsp water

2 tsp sugar/sweetener

1 tsp cinnamon

30g/1oz raisins

1 tsp honey

60g/2oz medium fat cream cheese

1 egg

2 tbsp milk

METHOD

1. Heat up 1 tsp of the coconut oil in a saucepan and gently cook the chopped apples. After around 5 minutes, add the raisins, cinnamon, sugar/sweetener, water and honey. Gently simmer until the apples have softened – this should take around 10 minutes.

2. Cut the lavash bread into 4 portions. Spread around 15g of the cheese on each, together with a quarter of the apple filling. Roll each one into a cylinder.

3. Beat the egg and add in the milk. Pour this mixture into a shallow dish and dip in the rolls. Leave each one to soak for a few minutes.

4. Heat up the remaining coconut oil and fry the rolls on high heat for around 4 minutes, or until golden brown.

| 150 CALORIES | 7g PROTEIN | 5g FAT | 25g CARBS |

MACROS (PER ROLL)

PROTEIN BALLS make great snacks to eat on-the-go.
Making them is simple – all you really need is the following:
- protein powder
- something sweet (e.g. sweetener, honey, dates)
- something sticky to hold everything together (e.g. peanut butter, coconut oil, dates)
- whatever else you want to add

On the next pages you will find four tasty ideas (the salted caramel balls are my personal favourite). Once you've got the hang of these, you will be able to conjure up your own combinations.....let me know what you come up with.

SALTED CARAMEL PROTEIN BALLS

MAKES 6 BALLS

5 MINS PREP

INGREDIENTS
6 medjool dates
50g/½ cup/2 scoops unflavoured whey protein
2 tbsp water
1/2 tsp salted caramel flavouring (optional)
20g/¾oz chopped nuts

120 CALORIES 8g PROTEIN 2g FAT 19g CARBS

MACROS (PER BALL)

METHOD

1. Carefully roast the chopped nuts in a frying pan (no need for any oil) until browned. Keep aside.

2. Remove the stones from the medjool dates and add, together with the whey protein, water and salted caramel flavouring (if using), into a food processor.

3. Blend until fully combined.

4. Divide the mixture into 6 balls and roll in the mixed nuts to cover.

CHOCOLATE CHIP COOKIE DOUGH PROTEIN BALLS

MAKES 8 BALLS

5 MINS PREP

INGREDIENTS
50g/½ cup/1 scoop vanilla whey protein
4 tbsp milk
2 heaped tbsp (40g) almond butter
2 tbsp ground almonds
2 tbsp coconut flour
30g/1oz chocolate chips

115 CALORIES 8g PROTEIN 8g FAT 4g CARBS

MACROS (PER BALL)

METHOD

1. Mix together the vanilla whey, almond butter, ground almonds and coconut flour. Add in the milk gradually – you may need a little more or little less depending on how runny the almond butter is. The mixture should be soft but not too sticky to handle (if it becomes too sticky, simply add a little more of any of the dry ingredients or chill in the fridge).

2. Divide into 8 balls and push in the chocolate chips.

CHOCOLATE GOJI PROTEIN BALLS

MAKES 8 BALLS

10 MINS PREP

INGREDIENTS
25g/1oz coconut oil
25g/1oz dark chocolate
25g/1oz goji berries
1 tsp sugar/sweetener
50ml/3 tbsp hot water
50g/½ cup/2 scoops unflavoured whey protein
1 tbsp cocoa powder (plus extra for rolling)
25g/1oz fine oats

MACROS (PER BALL)

METHOD

1. Melt the coconut oil and dark chocolate together in a saucepan on a very low heat, taking care not to burn the chocolate. Leave to cool.

2. Add the hot water and sugar/sweetener to the goji berries and leave for 15 minutes or so to rehydrate the berries.

3. Once both the berries/hot water and chocolate/coconut oil mixtures have cooled, mix together and add the oats, cocoa powder and vanilla whey.

4. Roll into balls and cover in cocoa powder.

SUPERFOOD PROTEIN BALLS

MAKES 8 BALLS

5 MINS PREP

INGREDIENTS
100g/3½oz cooked quinoa
50g/½ cup/2 scoops vanilla whey
2 tbsp milk
2 tbsp peanut butter
1 tsp honey
1 tbsp chia seeds
1 tbsp pumpkin/sunflower seeds
1 tbsp dried cranberries

MACROS (PER BALL)

METHOD

1. Mix together the cooked quinoa, vanilla whey, milk, peanut butter and honey until well blended.

2. Shape into 8 balls.

3. Pour out the seeds/cranberries onto a plate and roll around the balls to coat.
.

CHOCOLATE CHIP
PROTEIN COOKIES

MAKES 8 MINI COOKIES

10 MINS PREP
10 - 15 MINS BAKING

INGREDIENTS

25g/¼ cup/1 scoop pea protein

½ cup/50g oats

100ml/7 tbsp milk

1 tbsp almond butter

1 tbsp coconut oil, melted

3 tbsp sugar/sweetener

15g/½oz chocolate chips

METHOD

1. Preheat the oven to 180°C/350°F. Line a baking tray with greaseproof paper.

2. Combine the pea protein, oats, milk, almond butter, coconut oil and sugar/sweetener. Mix well.

3. Spoon the mixture onto the baking tray (you should be able to make 8 small cookies), flatten and press a couple of chocolate chips into each cookie.

4. Bake for 10 – 15 minutes, until they are *just* cooked.

Recipe notes:
* *Be careful not to overbake the cookies....
they will taste much better undercooked
than overcooked.*

 110 CALORIES **6g** PROTEIN **5g** FAT **9g** CARBS

MACROS (PER COOKIE)

PROTEIN
MINCE PIES

MAKES 12

20 MINS PREP
45 MINS COOKING

INGREDIENTS

for the 'mincemeat':

2 medium apples

1 tbsp coconut oil

150g/5⅓ oz dried fruit

1/2 cup water

1 tsp sugar/sweetener

1 tsp vanilla extract

1 tsp ground ginger

1 tsp cinnamon

for the pastry:

50g/½ cup/2 scoops pea protein

100g/3½ wholemeal self-raising flour

(plus extra for dusting)

60g/½ cup ground almonds

150g/5⅓oz plain yoghurt

2 egg whites

1 tbsp sugar/sweetener

METHOD

1. Firstly make the 'mincemeat': remove the cores and chop the apples into small pieces. Melt the coconut oil in a small saucepan and add the apple pieces. Fry for a few minutes, stirring constantly.

2. Add the remaining mincemeat ingredients and stir. Simmer for around 30 minutes, adding more water if the mixture begins to dry out.

3. Preheat the oven to 180°C/350°F and grease a 12-hole muffin pan and a separate baking tray.

4. Using a food processor, combine the pastry ingredients until they form a dough.

5. Tip out onto a lightly floured surface and knead the dough until it becomes firm enough to roll.

6. Roll out the dough as thin as possible using either your hands or a rolling pin. Using a round cutter or a cup, cut out 12 bases and place them into the greased muffin trays. Using a star cutter (or a knife if you don't have one), cut out 12 stars and place onto the greased baking tray.

7. Bake for 10 – 15 minutes, or until lightly browned.

8. Remove the mince pie bases from the oven and spoon in some 'mincemeat' into each one. Place a star on top and serve.

Recipe notes:

- *Depending on how thick the yoghurt you use is (I used Skyr), the pastry may need a little more or less (if you put in too much, just add more of one of the dry ingredients).*

- *The pastry would also make a great pizza base or quiche crust (just add a pinch of sugar/sweetener rather than a tablespoon for a more savoury pastry).*

- *If you have some oranges or lemons handy, a little grated zest in the mincemeat would be lovely. As would a shot of brandy.*

 150 CALORIES
 8g PROTEIN
 4g FAT
 19g CARBS

MACROS (PER MINCE PIE)

PROTEIN EGGNOG

SERVES 3

10 MINS PREP

INGREDIENTS

250ml/1 cup milk

25g/¼ cup/1 scoop vanilla whey

1 cinnamon stick

½ tsp freshly grated nutmeg (plus extra for serving).

2 eggs, separated

1 tbsp sugar/sweetener

a shot of rum (optional)

METHOD

1. Add the vanilla whey and milk into a protein shaker and shake well to combine.

2. Pour into a small saucepan and add the cinnamon stick and nutmeg. Heat very gently – do not bring to the boil. Remove from the heat just before it reaches the point of boiling and leave to steep.

3. Using a handheld whisk, beat the egg yolks and sugar/sweetener until combined and thick.

4. Combine this egg yolk mixture with the whey mixture and stir until combined and smooth. Add the rum, if using, and leave in the fridge to cool.

5. Before serving, beat the egg whites with an electric whisk until soft peaks form. Gently fold this into the eggnog.

6. Serve with grated nutmeg on top.

Recipe notes:

- Be careful not to overheat the whey, it will curdle.

- Eggnog is traditionally made with cream, which tastes great but makes the calorie and fat count shoot up. You can add some double cream to this recipe if you want, it will taste amazing.

- The shot of rum is optional but **highly** recommended.

150 CALORIES 14g PROTEIN 6g FAT 9g CARBS

MACROS (PER SERVING)

CHRISTMAS PROTEIN PANCAKES

MAKES 8 PANCAKES
SERVES 2

5 MINS PREP
10 MINS COOKING

INGREDIENTS

25g/¼ cup/1 scoop unflavoured whey

25g/¼ cup/1 scoop fine oats

1 medium ripe banana

1 egg + 2 egg whites

a handful of spinach

1 tsp baking powder

2 tsp coconut oil

METHOD

1. Place all of the ingredients except for the coconut oil in a food processor and mix them together.

2. Heat half of the coconut oil up in a frying pan on low-medium heat and carefully spoon in 4 circles of batter.

3. Flip over once browned (this should only take a few minutes) and remove from the pan once the 2nd side is done.

4. Add the remaining oil and repeat.

Recipe notes:

- *Who needs green food colouring when you have spinach?? You won't even be able to taste it.*

- *You can of course leave the spinach out or, if it's nowhere near Christmas time, call them 'Hulk' pancakes.*

 240 CALORIES
 20g PROTEIN
 9g FAT
 24g CARBS

MACROS (PER SERVING)

PROTEIN BISCUITS

MAKES 5 BISCUITS

5 MINS PREP

10 - 15 MINS BAKING

INGREDIENTS

100g/1 cup ground almonds (plus a little extra for dusting)

25g/¼ cup/1 scoop pea protein

1 tbsp water

5 medjool dates, stones removed

1 egg white

METHOD

1. Heat the oven to 170°C/340°F. Line a baking tray with some greaseproof paper.

2. Put all of the ingredients in a food processor and mix thoroughly until the dates have completely broken down and the mixture has become a firm dough.

3. Sprinkle some ground almonds on a clean surface and flatten the dough, using your hands, until it is around half a centimetre thick.

4. Using a cookie cutter, cut out 5 shapes (you will probably have to shape the last one using your hands) and place on the baking tray.

5. Bake for 10 – 15 minutes, or until the biscuits have turned golden brown.

Recipe notes:

• Anything with ground nuts in will burn very easily, so be sure to bake at a low oven temperature and keep an eye on the biscuits.

• If you don't want to use expensive ground almonds for dusting, any kind of flour will do.

• If you want to use these as tree decorations as I have, use a cocktail stick to make a hole in each biscuit before baking for the silver thread to fit through. Decorate with some instant icing (not included in the macros sadly..).

 195 CALORIES
 10g PROTEIN
 11g FAT
 12g CARBS

MACROS (PER BISCUIT)

PROTEIN BANANA BREAD

MAKES 10 SLICES

10 MINS PREP
50 – 60 MINS BAKING

INGREDIENTS

4 medium bananas

50g/½ cup/2 scoops unflavoured whey

100g/1 cup ground almonds

50g/½ cup coconut flour

1 tsp baking powder

60g/½ cup walnut pieces

2 eggs

METHOD

1. Preheat the oven to 180°C/350°F. Grease a 20cm/8in loaf tin.

2. Combine three of the bananas with all of the other ingredients. Mash the banana roughly (don't worry about getting it completely smooth – the lumps will taste good) but make sure everything else is blended.

3. Spoon the mixture into the loaf tin. Slice the remaining banana into two lengthways and place over the top.

4. Bake for 50 – 60 minutes.

Recipe notes:

• This is a flourless recipe, which means that the result is a little softer and heavier than regular banana bread. You could always replace some of the ground almonds with plain flour for a more 'cake'-like texture.

• The riper the bananas are, the sweeter the finished banana bread will be.

• The addition of the walnut pieces is highly recommended....however, if you leave them out, you will save 40 calories and 4g of fat per slice.

200 CALORIES   **10g** PROTEIN   **12g** FAT   **18g** CARBS

MACROS (PER SLICE)

PROTEIN
S'MORES IN A MUG

MAKES 1

10 MINS PREP
5 MINS COOKING

INGREDIENTS

for the hot chocolate:

25g/¼ cup/1 scoop unflavoured whey

70ml/⅓ cup milk

1 tbsp cashew butter

1 tbsp cocoa

1 tbsp sugar/sweetener

for the cookie:

4 tbsp ground almonds (plus a little extra for dusting)

1 tsp pea protein

1 medjool date, stone removed

1 tsp egg white

6 mini marshmallows

METHOD

1. Firstly, make the cookie: place the cookie ingredients into a food processor and mix until a dough is formed. Remove the dough from the food processor and keep aside.

2. Next, place all of the hot chocolate ingredients into the food processor (no need to clean it) and mix until a thick chocolaty syrup is formed. Pour this out into a mug.

3. Gently heat the hot chocolate mixture in the microwave, being very careful not to let it reach boiling point (heat up in 10 second bursts).

4. Shape the biscuit dough into a round shape and place on top of the hot chocolate. Push in the mini marshmallows and place under a hot grill for a few minutes, until the biscuit is lightly toasted and the marshmallows are melted.

Recipe notes:

• This is a very indulgent treat for one. The protein hot chocolate is very good on its own and has only 235 calories, 26g protein, 12g fat and 12g carbs.

• Be careful not to overheat the hot chocolate; the whey will curdle.

 446 CALORIES
 36g PROTEIN
 23g FAT
 29g CARBS

MACROS

SALTED CHILLI-CHOCOANANA BITES

MAKES 16

15 MINS PREP

1.5 HOURS CHILLING TIME

INGREDIENTS

1 ripe banana

50g/½ cup/2 scoops vanilla whey protein

80g/1 cup oats

2 tbsp almond butter

to coat:

100g/3½oz dark chocolate

1 tbsp coconut oil

sea salt

red chilli flakes

METHOD

1. Mash the banana and combine with 60g of the oats, the vanilla whey and almond butter.

2. Sprinkle the remaining oats over a plate and use them as a dusting to help you to shape the mixture into a big rectangle. Freeze for 1 - 2 hours.

3. Melt the chocolate and coconut oil together.

4. Cut the banana/oat mixture into squares and dip each one into the chocolate/coconut oil.

5. Sprinkle each square with sea salt & chilli flakes and chill in the fridge for 30 minutes to allow the chocolate to set.

Recipe notes:

• *This recipe is by my friend Willy Wong. Take a look at his Instagram (@willy_w0ngka) for loads more great recipes.*

• *The sea salt and chilli flakes are optional, and you can make the banana/oat mixture into bars rather than bites if you wish.*

110 CALORIES 5g PROTEIN 5g FAT 11g CARBS

MACROS (PER BITE)

PROTEIN ICECREAM

SERVES 2

5 MINS PREP
1 – 1½ HOURS FREEZING TIME

INGREDIENTS

250ml/8.5 fl oz Fat Free Greek Yoghurt

25ml/¼ cup/1 scoop vanilla whey

2 tsp cocoa powder

1 tsp sugar/sweetener

METHOD

1. Mix all of the ingredients together and pour into a large plastic tub.

2. Place the tub in the freezer and, after around 20 minutes, stir the mixture rapidly with a fork or spatula to break it up.

3. Repeat 2 or 3 times, stirring every 20 minutes or so, until the mixture is smooth and creamy. If the mixture becomes too hard, simply place into the fridge until it becomes soft enough to stir.

4. Once the mixture is fully frozen and ice cream-like, serve.

Recipe notes:

• Any kind of tub or container with a large surface area can be used for this recipe.

• You can add whatever you want into the ice-cream mix: chocolate chips, crumbled brownie pieces, fruit....you can even change the flavour completely by using a different kind of protein powder.

125 CALORIES **23g** PROTEIN **1g** FAT **7g** CARBS

MACROS (PER SERVING)

CHOCOLATE PROTEIN CRISPIES

MAKES 8

10 MINS PREP
1 HOUR CHILLING TIME

INGREDIENTS

50g/1¾oz chocolate

1 tbsp coconut oil

75g/2½oz peanut butter

50g/½ cup/2 scoops unflavoured whey

50g/1¾oz whey protein crispies

METHOD

1. Melt the chocolate together with the coconut oil and peanut butter gently in a saucepan on a low heat.

2. Once melted and cooled completely, add in the whey powder and whey protein crispies. Mix everything together and spoon into a brownie tin lined with greaseproof paper.

3. Leave in the fridge to set for at least an hour.

4. Cut into 8 pieces and serve.

Recipe notes:
- *Whey protein crispies are available from most of the big online protein stores. If you can't get hold of them, you can use rice crispies instead which, surprisingly, doesn't change the macros that much.*

 150 CALORIES **12g** PROTEIN **10g** FAT **7g** CARBS

MACROS (PER CRISPIE)

ACKNOWLEDGEMENTS

This book wouldn't exist without the support of the following people:

My parents Margaret and Frank – thank you for putting up with me and for your help with proofreading.

My son Ale – thank you for being the best son in the world and for being a great hand model for the s'mores in a mug recipe.

Willy Wong – thanks for being my biggest fan (the feeling is mutual) and for allowing me to use two of your great recipes and images.

AJ Silvers – thank you for being a huge inspiration and for believing in me. This book simply wouldn't have ever got finished if it wasn't for you.

Mark Runza - thanks so much for letting me use one of your recipes. Your app is amazing.

Sheryl Dickie – thank you for believing in me when I didn't even believe in myself. It really helped.

Dan Meredith – you are probably too busy running your empire to ever use a cookbook but thank you for all you have done for me. I'll always be a big fan.

Kay Smith – thanks for all your patience (yet again!). I'm not sure if I'll ever be a super-organised person and get things ready in time.